The Little Book
of
Game of Thrones
Facts

The Fact Bomb Company Limited

D0064039

eBook – ISBN 978-1-78926-849-2

Paperback – ISBN 978-1-78926-848-5

Please feel free to follow us on social media for future books and daily fun facts!

Instagram – https://www.instagram.com/thefactbombcompany/

Facebook – https://www.facebook.com/The-Fact-Bomb-Company-334831483939843

Twitter - https://twitter.com/bomb_fact

YouTube - https://www.youtube.com/channel/UCmAfXGTX5M98KoU5tW224jQ?

DEDICATION

"Facts are stubborn things; and whatever may be our wishes, our inclinations, or the dictates of our passion, they cannot alter the state of facts and evidence." - John Adams.

The Fact Bomb Company was founded in the belief that facts make the world a better place. We are passionate in our mission to provide facts to people in a way that they can enjoy them and expand their knowledge.

This book, like all our books, is dedicated to all those people who seek greater knowledge through facts.

CONTENTS

ACKNOWLEDGMENTS

We at The Fact Bomb Company would like to acknowledge the creative genius that is George RR Martin. His stories continue to inspire and amaze millions of people around the world. We thank you George.

1. THE AUTHOR

1. George Raymond Martin was born on the 20th September 1948 in Bayonne New Jersey. He later adopted the middle name Richard at age thirteen to become known as George Raymond Richard Martin (GRRM).

2. The majority of Martin's childhood was spent living in federal housing projects with his two younger sisters, Darleen and Janet. This relatively poor upbringing resulted in the young Martin using his imagination to escape to exciting alternative worlds, each filled with mythical creatures, kingdoms and treacherous plots. These early imaginative ideas were written down and sold for pennies to his classmates. Many involved his pet turtles.

3. Martin had a keen interest in comic books growing up and wrote fiction for various fanzines during his teenage years. He cited the death of the Avengers character Wonder Man, who dies in his first story, as sparking his interest in tragic doomed characters.

4. He studied journalism at Northwester University's Medill School of Journalism, earning a bachelor's degree.

5. A conscientious objector during the Vietnam War, Martin avoided the conflict and instead served as a volunteer for a legal assistance foundation.

6. Post University, Martin taught English and journalism for a while at Clarke University but the death of his friend and author Tom Reamy in 1977 resulted in him taking the fateful decision to become a full-time writer.

7. Martin began selling science fiction short stories in 1970, the first of which was titled "The Hero".

8. Throughout the next two decades, he wrote multiple books in the science fiction genre and moved to Hollywood to write for the more lucrative world of television.

9. Martin is a fan of role-playing games (RPGs) and admits he lost a year from writing in 1983 through playing the game Superworld.

10. Martin is twice married, first to Gale Burnick (1975-1979) and then to longtime partner Parris McBride (2011-present).

11. He considers himself to be atheist or agnostic.

12. Martin is a keen fan of both the New York Jets American football team and the New York Mets baseball team.

13. 💣 Martin once said, if he was to be a Game of Thrones character it would be that of Samwell Tarly.

2. A SONG OF ICE AND FIRE NOVELS

1. "A Game of Thrones" (GoT) is the first novel in GRRM's fantasy series "A Song of Ice and Fire".

2. While many think of Game of Thrones as a fairly recent phenomenon, the original book was actually released in 1996. The novel won the 1997 Locus Award which is presented by the fantasy magazine Locus. It was also nominated for various other awards, including the World Fantasy Award.

3. It wasn't until July 2011 that *A Game of Thrones* became a New York Times bestseller, reaching number one.

4. The second book released was "A Clash of Kings" which was published in November 1998 in the United Kingdom. As per his first novel, *A Clash of Kings* won the Locus Award for Best Novel.

5. Continuing the two year release cycle, Martin released "A Storm of Swords" in August 2000 in the United Kingdom.

6. As *A Storm of Swords* was so long, the paperback addition was split into two parts in many regions and in France it was split into four parts. The third book continued the run of success by also winning the 2001 Locus Award.

7. In 2005 GRRM released the fourth novel in the series "A Feast of Crows". Given the volume of material with which Martin had to work, he decided to split the material by character and

location, resulting in two novels being published simultaneously with different casts of characters. "A Feast of Crows" was the first of these two simultaneous novels released.

8. *A Feast of Crows* became the first book of the series to achieve widespread success as it debuted at number one in the New York Times Sci-Fi bestseller list.

9. It was not until 2011 that the second simultaneous published book was released, entitled "A Dance with Dragons". This was the first book released following the start of the HBO television series "Game of Thrones".

10. *A Dance with Dragons* (US Hardcover), encompasses 1040 pages and is the longest of the current five published GoT novels.

11. GRRM had a bet with his friend Patrick St. Denis that if the New York Giants did not have a better season than the Dallas Cowboys, he would add Patrick as a character in his book and have him killed by giants. Martin lost the bet and , in *A Dance with Dragons,* a character called "Sir Patrick of King's Mountain" is slain by giants.

12. The final two novels are to be titled "The Winds of Winter" and "A Dream of Spring". GRRM believes both novels will be over 1,500 pages in length.

13. A release date has not currently been set for either book.

14. Martin originally envisaged the books as a trilogy but, to date (2018), he has published five of seven expected volumes.

15. The books are inspired by the War of the Roses, which were a series of English civil wars fought for control of the throne of England between the House of Lancaster (red rose) and the house of York (white rose).

16. Martin dislikes modern technology in order to write his novels, preferring to type them using WordStar 4.0

17. The novels have been translated into more than 47 different languages.

18. **As of August 2018, the novel titled** *A Song of Ice and Fire* has sold more than 90 million copies worldwide, including 45 million in the United States.

19. 💣 Every character in the books who has had a point of view in the epilogue or prologue has died.

3. THE TELEVISION SERIES

1. The Red Wedding might be brutal but without it there may possibly never have been a follow up television show. Executive producers David Benioff and D.B Weiss decided to create the show after reading about the Red Wedding in the books.

2. The pilot episode was never aired on television and was widely rejected by critics.

3. The books only contain a few examples of Dothraki and this was expanded upon for the television show to create a language of over 2000 words.

4. Tyrion Lannister has the most appearances in the TV series up to season seven, featuring in 58 out of a possible 64 episodes.

5. Game of Thrones is known for being bloody and for good reason. During the first seven seasons, there have only been five episodes in which there have been no deaths on screen.

6. Sophie Turner, who plays Sansa Stark, adopted her direwolf Lady character after she was killed in Season One.

7. Dean-Charles Chapman, who played Tommen Baratheon from Season Four onwards, previously played Martyn Lannister in Season Three. He only appears briefly in this season before being killed by Lord Karstark.

8. The three dragon eggs in the show were presented to GRRM by the show's producers.

9. In the first seven seasons of Game of Thrones there have been ten actors who have appeared in Harry Potter and eight who have appeared in Star Wars. How many can you name?

10. GRRM famously texted Jack Gleeson, who plays Joffrey, "Congratulations on your marvelous performance. Everyone hates you!"

11. Actor Kristian Nairn is a DJ when he is not playing the lovable Hodor.

12. Kristian Nairn is 6ft 10in tall.

13. Peter Dinklage, who plays Tyrion Lannister, is only 4ft 5in tall.

14. Lena Headey, who plays Cersei, did not do the walk of atonement as it was carried out by a body double. Shame!

15. A number of musicians have appeared in cameo roles including Snow Patrol, Coldplay, Sigur Ros, Of Monsters and Men, Bastille and Ed Sheeran.

16. The most expensive death in the television series to date was during the scene where Arya killed Ser Meryn Trant in a brothel. Apparently eye gouging CGI is very expensive.

17. Iwan Rheon, who is best known for playing Ramsey Bolton, originally auditioned for the role of Jon Snow.

18. The heart eaten by Daenerys was actually made out of gummy candy.

19. The Night's Watch cloaks in the show are actually rugs from Ikea. The company now offer instructions about how to turn their rugs into a Night's Watch cape.

20. Peter Vaughan, who plays Maester Aemon, was also partially blind in real life.

21. In the scene where Ned Stark's head is on a spike, if you look closely, in the background there is former President George W. Bush's head also on a spike. A formal apology was issued following this and newer versions have had it digitally removed.

22. The Dothraki are often thought to be modelled on the Mongols. An example of this is the molten gold poured onto Visery's head by Khal Drogo, as similarly, in the 13th century it is rumoured the Mongols killed Inalchuq, the governor of Otrar, by pouring molten silver into his eyes and ears.

23. Game of Thrones has been banned by the Turkish military to protect people from "pornography and exhibitionism" amongst other things.

24. A number of famous actors and actresses turned down parts in Game of Thrones in its early days including Gillian Anderson, Dominic West, Brian Cox and Jennifer Ehle.

25. Jonathan Pryce originally turned down an unnamed Game of Thrones role but finally agreed to appear in Season Five as the High Sparrow.

26. Maisie Williams, who plays Ayra Stark, is actually right handed but plays Ayra as left-handed. This makes those sword fight scenes even more impressive!

27. The term "sexposition" was coined by critic Myles McNutt to describe important plot points being divulged during intimate scenes in Game of Thrones.

28. Queen Elizabeth has visited the set of Game of Thrones but reportedly declined to sit on the Iron Throne.

29. HBO started selling replica Iron Thrones in 2012 for the princely sum of $30,000 , a King's Ransom indeed!

30. 💣 **George RR Martin has informed producers David Benioff and D.B Weiss regarding the ending to Game of Thrones.**

4. HOUSE STARK

1. House Stark was founded by Brandon the Builder and is over 8000 years old.

2. The House Sigil of the Starks is a direwolf and the seat of the house is Winterfell.

3. The house motto is "Winter is Coming" which makes it unique in terms of GoT mottos as it is not a boast or a threat.

4. The members of House Stark are descended from the first men, with many still following the old religion.

5. The house survived the Targaryen conquest when King Torrhen Stark surrendered to the Targaryen army and was made "Lord Paramount of the North".

6. As a result of the Stark surrender, there is no Stark sword in the Iron Throne.

7. At the time of writing this book, the de facto Lord is Jon Snow and Sansa Stark is the official Lord given the illegitimacy of Jon's birth.

8. The heir is Arya Stark.

9. The full military strength of House Stark and it's vassals is 45,000 men.

10. House Stark was heavily involved in Robert's Rebellion as it began with Prince Rhaegar Targaryen kidnapping Lyanna Stark. This led to Lord Rickard Stark and, his son and heir, Brandon Stark demanding her return. They paid for this demand with their lives.

11. Eddard Stark led an army featuring Houses Stark, Baratheon, Tully and Arryn into war with the Targaryens.

12. After victories at the Battle of the Bells and Battle of the Trident, Eddard Stark led his forces to Kings Landing to take the Iron Throne.

13. Eddard Stark declined the Iron Throne in order to allow friend and ally Robert Baratheon to rule.

14. Eddard Stark has six children, of whom five have Catelyn of House Tully as their mother.

15. Robert, Sansa, Rickon and Bran all have the auburn hair and blue eyes of the Tullys while Jon and Ayra have the long dark hair and grey eyes of the Starks.

16. Jon Snow's direwolf is called Ghost and this name foreshadowed Jon's later death and resurrection.

17. The Stark's gifted Bear Island to the Mormont family after it was won from the Greyjoys.

18. Direwolfs were a historic species similar to modern grey wolves. They became extinct approximately 10,000 years ago.

19. ● According to Old Nan in the books, the **Night King is a Stark and was 13th Commander of the Nights Watch.**

5. HOUSE LANNISTER

1. House Lannister was founded by Lann the Clever who lived to the age of 312 and had a hundred sons and a hundred daughters.

2. The house sigil is a golden lion and the ancestral seat of the house is Casterly Rock which was deceitfully taken from its previous owners by Lann the Clever.

3. The official house motto is actually "Hear me Roar" and not the commonly used "A Lannister always pays his debts".

4. At the time of writing this book, the Lord of House Lannister is disputed between Cersei and Tyrion. The heir is Ser Jaime Lannister.

5. The family are the wealthiest in Westeros due to their ownership of the gold and silver mines in the Westerlands.

6. Forbes once ranked Tywin Lannister's wealth at $2.1 billion dollars on their fictional Rich List.

7. The Lannisters are descended from the Andals and are known for being fair-haired, tall and handsome.

8. The full military strength of House Lannister and its vassals is 20,000 men.

9. The family sword , called Brightroar , was made of Valyrian steel. It was taken by Tommen II to Valyria after the Doom and was never seen again. This is partly the reason the Lannisters were so happy to melt down Ned Stark's great sword after his death.

10. Tywin's brother Gerion sailed to Valyria to find the sword but never returned.

11. House Clegane was founded when Tytos Lannister was about to be eaten by a lion but was saved by the Lannister's kennel master. Tytos granted the kennel master lands and promoted him into gentry, during which process House Clegane was created.

12. It is not only Jaime and Cersei who like to keep things in the family. Tywin Lannister married his first cousin, Joanna Lannister.

13. King Aerys took liberties during Tywin's wedding ceremony to Joanna.

14. Tywin Lannister had originally planned for Cersei to marry Prince Rhaegar Targaryen. The request was rejected by King Aerys who called Tywin a servant.

15. Jaime was meant to marry Lysa Tully but decided to become a Kingsguard instead. Tywin then offered Tyrion instead but Hoster Tully rejected him because of his dwarfism.

16. 💣 The Rains of Castamere was a song written to immortalise the defeat of House Reyne by House Lannister. At the end of the war Tywin Lannister flooded the caves under Castamere holding the last members of House Reyne, killing them all.

6. HOUSE TARGARYEN

1. The official house motto is "Fire and Blood".

2. The house sigil is a three headed dragon.

3. At the time of writing this book, the Lord of House Targaryen is Daenerys Targaryen.

4. The house seat is Dragonstone which the family have occupied for over five hundred years.

5. Military strength comprises of 100,000 Dothraki, 8,000 Unsullied and two dragons.

6. Targaryens are known for their white or silver hair, pale skin and eye colour which ranges from blue to purple.

7. They are also known to have dreams which can foretell the future.

8. Aegon the Conqueror was the Targaryen leader who invaded Westeros.

9. He was responsible for the building of Kingslanding, the Red Keep and the Iron Throne.

10. He had two sisters who were also his wives, namely Visenya and Rhaenys.

11. Aegon invaded with three dragons; Balerion, Vhagar and Meraxes.

12. Balerion was the largest of the dragons and forged the Iron Throne with his breath. He died of natural causes at the age 200 and his skull is stored in the Red Keep.

13. Vhagar was ridden by Aegon's sister-wife Visenya and was killed at the Battle Above the Gods Eye. Like Balerion, her skull is also stored in the Red Keep.

14. Meraxes was ridden by Aegon's other sister-wife Rhaenys. She was killed at the Siege of Helliholt and her skull is also stored in the Red Keep.

15. Dragons can only be hatched by "fire and blood", which is why Daenerys burns the witch with the dragon eggs.

16. It takes four years for newly hatched Dragons to reach the size of ponies and they never stop growing as long as they live.

17. Dragons are of no fixed sex and can switch between male and female.

18. The weak spot in a Dragon's armour is through its eyes.

19. House Blackfyre is a house founded by the bastard son of Aegon, Daemon Blackfyre. They feature in the books but are largely omitted from the television series.

20. The Kingsguard was created by the Targaryens.

21. Daenerys got the name "Stormborn" because she was born during a powerful storm that destroyed the Targaryen fleet.

22. She is able to speak five languages; Common Tongue, Dothraki, Chiscari, High Valerian and Bastard Valerian.

23. Daenerys is not actually "first of her name" as there was a previous Princess Daenerys who was the daughter of King Aegon IV.

24. Jon Snow is the nephew of Daenerys because his father was Prince Rhaegar Targaryen.

25. 💣 **Despite what is shown in the television show, Targaryens are not immune to fire and Daenerys escaping injury is more likely to do with magic than any immunity.**

7. HOUSE TYRELL

1. House Tyrell was founded by Alester Tyrell.

2. The house sigil is golden rose on a green field. The rose signifies the outwardly nice projection of House Tyrell but remember roses also have thorns!

3. The official house motto is "Growing Strong".

4. At the time of writing this book, there is sadly no obvious Lord or Heir after the house was wiped out by wildfire in the Great Sept of Baelor.

5. The house seat is Highgarden which is situated in The Reach region. House Tyrell came to rule here after the previous rulers of The Reach, House Gardener, were wiped out during the Targaryen conquest.

6. The Reach is the most populous region of Westeros and it also produces more food than it eats, with the excess being exported to other houses.

7. At the height of their powers, House Tyrell could rely on a military strength of over a 100,000 men which was the largest army in Westeros.

8. The Citadel sits within Tyrell lands as Oldtown is within the seat of House Hightower who are loyal bannermen to the House Tyrell.

9. 💣 **During Robert's rebellion, House Tyrell fought on the side of the Targaryens and inflicted the only defeat Robert suffered during the war at the Battle of Ashford.**

8. HOUSE BARATHEON

1. The official house motto is "Ours Is the Fury"

2. The house sigil is a stag with a crown on a gold background. The crown was added by King Robert once he ascended the throne.

3. The sigil and words were taken from the defeated House Durrandon and from which the maternal line of House Baratheon is descended.

4. At the time of writing this book, there is no Lord or Heir to House Baratheon. Gendry, King Robert's bastard, is the last known member of the family with blood ties.

5. The house seat is Storm's end which is in the Stormlands region. This region was given that name because of the frequent storms that affect the east coast of Westeros.

6. The characteristics of Baratheon's are tall, powerfully built with black hair and blue eyes. It was Geoffrey's lack of black hair that first aroused Ned Stark's suspicions that he wasn't a true Baratheon.

7. The house was founded by Orys Baratheon who was a general in the army of King Aegon I Targaryen.

8. Orys Baratheon defeated the last of the Storm Kings, Argilac the Arrogant, and captured Storm's End.

9. Orys was also rumored to be a bastard half-brother of Aegon Targaryen.

10. During fighting the Dornish, Orys was captured and had his right hand chopped off before being released after Aegon paid a ransom.

11. The house is 300 years old and was founded in 1 AC (After Conquest).

12. It was two-hundred and eighty-one years after being founded that House Baratheon assumed the throne after Lord Robert led a rebellion against King Aerys II Targaryen.

13. Robert Baratheon famously killed Prince Rhaegar Targaryen at the Battle of the Trident.

14. Robert was only nineteen years old at the time of the Rebellion.

15. The books and television series differ in terms of who was responsible for the murder of Robert's bastards. In the books Cersei gives the order but in the television series it is Geoffrey.

16. Robert and Stannis watched their parents drown off the coast of the Stormlands in a ferocious storm.

17. Stannis later claimed he lost his faith in the Seven on the day his parents drowned.

18. 💣 **The Baratheon's have Targaryen blood. Not only was it speculated that Orys was half Targaryen but in addition, his descendent Ormund Baratheon married Rhaelle Targaryen. One of the grandsons produced from this match was Robert Baratheon.**

9. HOUSE GREYJOY

1. The official house motto is actually "We Do Not Sow" and not the common saying "What Is Dead May Never Die".

2. The house sigil is a golden kraken on a black background.

3. The seat of House Greyjoy is Pyke which is located in the Iron Islands.

4. The house was founded by The Grey King.

5. The Grey King was said to have ruled the Iron Islands for a thousand years. The folk tales proclaim he took a mermaid for his wife.

6. The Grey King was also said to have fathered over one hundred sons and sixteen of those went on to found great Iron Born houses, including House Greyjoy.

7. The Greyjoy family became rulers after King Haren the Black was killed during the Targaryen conquest.

8. The current Lord is King Euron Greyjoy and there is no named heir.

9. Yara and Theon Greyjoy, daughter and son of previous King Balon, are open in rebellion against King Euron.

10. Those who live on the Iron Islands are often referred to as Iron Born.

11. Unlike most of Westeros, the Iron Born do not follow the Faith of the Seven and instead worship the Drowned God.

12. They Greyjoys rebelled during Robert's rule and Balon proclaimed the Kingdom of the Iron Islands.

13. The rebellion was ultimately crushed and two of Balon's three sons, Rodrik and Maron were killed. The third, Theon, was sent to live with Ned Stark as his ward.

14. At the height of their military power the Greyjoy's could boast a military strength of 15,000 men and one of the strongest fleets in the seven kingdoms.

15. The motto "We Do Not Sow" reflects the pillaging nature of the Iron Born. This is because they only reap i.e. pillage, and do not sow. When they pillage they pay for this using the "iron price" which is their blood.

16. Euron Greyjoy's ship is called Silence because he rips out the tongue of all his crew.

17. Euron has a horn called "Dragonbinder" which apparently can bind dragons to his will. The catch is that if the horn is blown it kills the user.

18. 💣 The Iron Born rulers are chosen using a form of democracy. A new king or queen is elected via Kingsmoot which is a gathering and vote on the new ruler.

10. HOUSE MARTELL

1. The official house motto is "Unbowed, Unbent, Unbroken".

2. The house sigil is a red sun which is pierced by a golden spear on an orange background.

3. The seat of House Martell is Sunspear which is located in Dorne.

4. The house, in its current form, was founded when local King Mors Martell married Queen Nymeria from Rhonye. They met when Nymeria and her people fled the Valyrian invasion of their homeland.

5. The marriage is seen in the sigil of House Martell with the golden spear of Mors Martell being combined with the red sun of Nymeria.

6. The Martell side of the family was founded by Andal warrior Morgan Martell.

7. The current lord is Ellaria Sand who, at the time of writing this book, is currently a prisoner of Cersei Lannister.

8. The Martells were the only great house not to be conquered during the Targaryen Conquest. This is reflected in the house words "Unbowed, Unbent, Unbroken".

9. They managed to defeat the Targaryens using guerilla warfare tactics.

10. The Targaryens tried again one-hundred and fifty years later under King Daeron I but after initial success the Targaryen army again was forced to withdraw.

11. The Martells were eventually brought into the fold of the seven kingdoms when King Daeron II married the sister of the Prince of Dorne and he in turn married Daeron II's sister.

12. The marriage bonds were strengthened later when King Aerys II Targaryen married his son Prince Rhaegar to Elia Martell. This marriage produced two children but all members of the family died in Robert's Rebellion.

13. The Dornish follow the traditions of the Rhoynar who have gender-equal succession in which the eldest child always assumes the throne regardless of sex.

14. The Martells also use the terms Prince and Princess for their rulers, a privilege which was granted to them through their Targaryen marriage alliances.

15. The Martells are dragon killers, having famously killed the great dragon Meraxes.

16. 💣 **The full house name of House Martell is actually "House Nymeros Martell". The Nymeros part refers to Queen Nymeria of Rhonye.**

11. HOUSE TULLY

1. The official house motto is "Family, Duty, Honor".

2. The house sigil is a silver trout jumping on a blue and red background.

3. The seat of House Tully is Riverrun which is located in the Riverlands region.

4. The current lord of House Tully is Edmure Tully and he has a son and heir.

5. The house was founded by Axel Tully who constructed the first castle at Riverrun. The castle has water on each side which makes it difficult to attack.

6. House Tully came to prominence during Aegon I's conquest when Edmyn Tully fought against Harren the Black who ruled the Riverlands. This act of support resulted in Edmyn being rewarded with the role of Lords Paramount of the Riverlands.

7. Hoster Tully and his brother Bryden Tully had a feud after Bryden refused to marry Bethany Redwyne. This resulted in Bryden breaking ties and being labelled "The Blackfish", a name which he later owned and used in his sigil.

8. Family members in House Tully tend to have fair skin, auburn hair and blue eyes.

9. When a member of the Tully family dies, they are placed in a small boat which is set afloat and then lit by a flaming arrow.

10. 💣 **During the Dance of the Dragons Targaryen civil war, the prominent members of House Tully are all named after Muppets; Lord Grover Tully, Ser Elmo Tully and Lord Kermit Tully!**

12. HOUSE ARRYN

1. The official house motto is "As High as Honor".

2. The house sigil is a white falcon and moon on a blue shield.

3. The seat of House Arryn is The Eyrie which is located in The Vale of Arryn.

4. The current Lord is Robin Arryn and the heir is Ser Harrold Hardyng.

5. House Arryn is one of the oldest houses as, according to legend, it was founded by Ser Artys Arryn who was known as the "Winged Knight". He founded the house after flying on top of a giant falcon and landing on the highest mountain in the Vale to defeat the King of the Mountain.

6. They managed to fight off the initial Targaryen invasion before finally surrendering. This voluntary surrender allowed the family to continue to reign as Lords Paramount of the Vale.

7. The Knights of the Vale are known as skilled horseback riders and at 45,000 men are one of the most powerful military factions in Westeros.

8. 💣 **The Eyrie is considered to be impregnable as it sits atop Giant's Lance which is the tallest mountain in the Vale.**

13. HOUSE FREY

1. The official house motto is "We Stand Together".

2. The house sigil is two stone towers and bridge on a grey background.

3. The seat of House Frey is The Twins which is located in the Riverlands region.

4. The Twins sits on the Trident river and is one of the primary crossing points. The Freys charge a toll to cross the river and this has made the family relatively wealthy.

5. The current Lord is unknown after Arya Stark assassinated Walder Frey and his two sons; Lothar and Walder.

6. The founder of House Frey is unknown but the house was founded three hundred years before the Targaryen conquest.

7. House Frey has only a small military force of 4,000 men but the strategic position of The Twins often means it is relied upon during the various wars.

8. Walder Frey was often referred to as the "Late Lord Frey" because he was late in joining Robert's rebellion and only showed up once the outcome had already been determined.

9.   💣   Walder Frey is known for his many wives and children. In the books he has had eight wives and thirty six children.

14. THE NIGHTS WATCH

1. The Night's Watch was founded over 8,000 years ago.

2. To show that its members are not bound to any houses, the Night's Watch does not have a heraldic symbol and instead use solid black on banners and shields.

3. The Night's Watch motto is ""Night gathers, and now my watch begins. It shall not end until my death. I shall take no wife, hold no lands, father no children. I shall wear no crowns and win no glory. I shall live and die at my post. I am the sword in the darkness. I am the watcher on the walls. I am the shield that guards the realms of men. I pledge my life and honor to the Night's Watch, for this night and all the nights to come."

4. The motto in the books contains the extra line "I am the fire that burns against the cold, the light that brings the dawn, the horn that wakes the sleepers".

5. This oath means that that members of the Night's Watch cannot marry, own land or father any children.

6.   The leader of the Night's Watch is called Lord Commander, currently this is Eddison Tollett.

7.   The youngest ever Lord Commander was Osric Stark who was ten years old when took the role.

8.   Jon Snow was the 998th Lord Commander.

9.   The military strength of the order is only 700 men. This is significantly less than the ten thousand at the time of Aegon Targaryen's invasion.

10. The Night's Watch man the wall and the castles that run along it, such as Castle Black and Eastwatch.

11. There were originally nineteen castles but many have been abandoned as successive rulers have spent less on the Night's Watch.

12. The wall is three hundred miles long and seven hundred feet high. It is almost entirely built from ice.

13. The wall in the series is based on real life Hadrian's Wall in Scotland which was built by the Romans to keep out the rebellious Scots.

14. There are three groups within the Night's Watch; the Rangers who fight and defend the wall, the Stewards who cook and clean, and the Builders who maintain the Wall and Castles.

15. Members have to wear all black which is why the Free Folk refer to them as "Crows".

16. Despite popular belief, members can leave the Night's Watch but only on the order of the ruling monarch.

17. 💣 **The Night's Watch have defeated the White Walkers before , during the Long Night. At the Battle for the Dawn, the Night's Watch fought alongside Azor Ahai to defeat the White Walkers.**

15. THE WHITE WALKERS

1. The White Walkers are thousands of years old and come from a time before the Age of Heroes.

2. The Children of the Forrest created the White Walkers to help protect them from the First Men who were killing them and stealing their lands.

3. The Children of the Forrest used magic to create the White Walkers from captured First Men. While originally able to control the White Walkers, The Children of the Forrest lost control of them.

4. The leader of the White Walkers is known as the Night King.

5. White Walkers are known for their glowing blue eyes.

6. The White Walkers can reanimate dead enemies who come back to life as wights. These wights serve as soldiers in the army of the dead.

7. This ability of White Walkers to reanimate the dead extends to animals, including Dragons!

8. A wight is difficult to kill as even decapitation has been shown to not destroy them. The two primary ways to kill them is either by fire or using dragonglass.

9. White Walkers are also difficult to kill but dragonglass and Valryian steel have been found effective.

10. When a White Walker is killed, any wights raised by them also die.

11. White Walkers are able to turn anything to ice which they touch and seem able to eliminate fire when they come into contact with it.

12. The White Walkers speak a language known as "Skroth" which sounds like cracking ice.

13. While not yet seen in the show, Westeros history makes reference to a female White Walker.

14. According to Old Nan, the White Walkers of the past rode giant spiders into battle.

10. 💣 **A person can only become a White Walker if the Night King is able to change them during infancy.**

16. RELIGION

1. The Old Gods of the Forest are a number of unnamed spirits of nature who were originally worshipped by the Children of the Forest. In more recent times, the Old Gods are primarily worshipped by those living in northern Westeros.

2. A godswood is an area within a castle keep which is centered on a heart tree, a giant weirwood with a face carved into the bark. This area is used to worship by those that follow the Old Gods.

3. Kingslaying, incest and not being hospitable to guests are deemed sins to those who follow the Old Gods.

4. The Faith of the Seven was brought to Westeros by the Andals. It is often referred to as the "New Gods" or simply "The Seven".

5. The Faith of the Seven believe in one god with seven faces. The seven faces are:

   a. The Father – representing justice

   b. The Mother – representing fertility

   c. The Maiden – representing innocence

   d. The Crone – representing wisdom

   e. The Warrior – representing strength

   f. The Smith – representing craftsmanship

   g. The Stranger – representing death

6. The Faith of the Seven uses a number of symbols and beliefs which relate to seven such as the seven pointed star or the fact that there are seven heavens and seven hells.

7. The New Gods are followed throughout most of Westeros and followers worship in seven sided temples or "Septs" as they are known. The most prominent of these was the Great Sept of Baelor.

8. The Drowned God is worshipped on the Iron Islands.

9. The Drowned God is the most violent of all Westeros religions as boys are not considered men until they have killed their first enemy.

10. The Drowned God is in a constant struggle with the Storm God, with the Drowned God located in the ocean and the Storm God in the sky.

11. Iron Born believe if they drown they feast on fish and are courted by mermaids in the halls of the Drowned God.

12. R'hllor is normally referred to the as the "Lord of Light" and this deity is worshipped as the Fire God or Red God.

13. The Fire God is not widely followed in Westeros but is a majority religion in several Free Cities to the east.

14. Those that follow R'hllor believe he is in a life and death struggle with the Great Other who represents darkness, death and the cold.

15. The Prince That Was Promised is a chosen warrior who Red God believers will come to combat the darkness in which the world currently lives.

16. Melisandre, also known as the Red Woman, is a Red Priestess of R'hllor. She is one of the oldest characters in the series at 401 years old.

17. The Many-Faced God is worshipped by the Faceless Men of Braavos. This god is sometimes referred to as the "God of Death".

18. Followers believe there to be only one Many-Faced God and the different gods of death followed by the other religions are actually all the same god, just with different faces.

19. The main temple to the God of Death is the House of Black and White located in Braavos.

20. The Great Stallion is the horse god worshipped by the Dothraki.

21. Similar to the Light of the Seven, the Dothraki also believe in a prophesied leader, theirs is called "The Stallion Who Mounts The World". This leader is believed to one day unite all Dothraki and help them conquer the world.

22. Widows of deceased Dothraki live in the city of Vaes Dothrak and are responsible for conducting religious rituals and interpreting omens.

11. 💣 The Dothraki follow "henotheism" which means that they only follow one god but do not deny that other gods exist.

17. THE LAWS AND CUSTOMS OF WESTEROS

1. The King's power is delegated throughout the land to the various Lords of Westeros. These Lords have the power to dispense justice over matters that occur within their lands.

2. Lords of Great Houses may further delegate judicial power to major or minor houses within their lands.

3. The relative degree of law and order in Westeros is often referred to as the "King's Peace".

4. The majority of Westeros does not have a resident police force but there are a few exceptions e.g. the City Watch in King's Landing.

5. There are various levels of Knighthood in the Seven Kingdoms:

    i. Hedge Knight – A freelance knight with no allegiance to a Lord.

    ii. Sworn Sword – A knight sworn in service to a particular Lord.

    iii. Landed Knight – A knight who has been given a small land holding by a Lord.

6. A Hedge Knight gets their name from the fact that they are considered so poor they often sleep under hedges while looking for employment.

7. Westeros society has a very clear class system which divides people into either commoners, also known lowborn, or nobles, also known as highborn.

8. The class to which belong defines the legal rights you possess as a citizen. For example, a noble has the right to demand trial by combat but a lowborn does not.

9. In highborn society men will always come before women in terms of inheritance, the exception to this being in Dorne.

10. Bastard children born into noble families are not eligible to inherit lands or titles but do receive the same legal benefits of their class.

11. Bastards are easily distinguished because they do not inherit the family name and instead are given a surname which signifies them as a bastard. These surnames differ depending on where the child was born:

    i.   Flowers – The Reach

    ii.   Hill – The Westerlands

    iii.   Pyke – The Iron Islands

    iv.   Rivers – The Riverlands

    v.   Sand – Dorne

    vi.   Snow – The North

    vii.   Stone – The Vale

    viii.   Storm – The Stormlands

    ix.   Waters – The Crownlands

12. The age at which a child legally becomes an adult is sixteen years old.

13. 💣 Marriages in the Seven Kingdoms are only legal if they have been consummated.

18. FINANCE, HEALTH AND HERALDRY

1. The currency used in the Seven Kingdoms is the Gold Dragon coin. This is supported by two smaller denomination coins: Silver Stag and Copper Penny.

2. When King Joffrey ascended the throne, the Seven Kingdoms were six million gold dragons in debt.

3. Medicine in Westeros is dispensed by Maesters who have had the necessary training. This is signified by a silver link in their chains.

4. Commoners often cannot afford the services of Maesters and will instead use wood's witches to cure illness using naturopathic remedies.

5. The main medical drugs used are essence of nightshade which is a sedative and milk of the poppy which is a painkiller.

6. In the Seven Kingdoms the noble houses use heraldry to distinguish themselves within society and on the battlefield.

7. It is illegal for a commoner to invent their own heraldry but once knighted, a commoner becomes a noble and therefore, may create their own heraldic design.

8. The most basic rule of heraldry is that of tincture. This rule states that metal should not be put on metal, nor colour on colour. What this means is metal colours e.g. gold and silver, cannot be put on top of each other and colours may also not be put on top of one another.

9. An exception to the tincture rule is that if the heraldry displays a real-world object, then this objects real colour can be used even if it does not meet the rules e.g. House Starks grey wolf on a white background.

10. Noble bastards cannot use the heraldry of their parent's house but can invent their own heraldry.

11. Wine is commonly drunk by the nobles in Westeros and the best is considered to be Arbor Gold.

12. The two main languages of Westeros are the Old Tongue and the Common Tongue. The Old Tongue is only really spoken by Wildlings.

13. Actors and entertainers in the Seven Kingdoms are called "mummers".

14. Mummers in the Seven Kingdoms do not give scripted performances and instead rely on more improvised acts or skills e.g. juggling or acrobatics.

15. 💣 **A troupe of mummers is not considered to be good unless they have a dwarf, who is often used for comedic effect.**

19. KEY ORGANISATIONS

1. The City Watch, also known as the "Gold Cloaks", are responsible for ensuring law and order in the capital.

2. The crown pays for the City Watch but the organisation swears no allegiance to the crown or any Lord.

3. There is no favouritism within the City Watch for those of noble birth and promotion is based on merit. The leader however, is referred to as "Lord Commander" if of noble birth and "Commander" if of common birth.

4. The Order of Maesters is an organisation of healers and scholars.

5. In reference to their intellect, Maesters are occasionally called the "Knights of the Mind".

6. The centre of the Order of the Maesters is The Citadel based in Oldtown.

7. Most noble families will have a resident Maester who is available to assist with a wider variety of tasks such as medicine, tutoring, political advice, weather prediction and communications via ravens.

8. Maesters, similar to the Night's Watch, are deemed servants of the realm and must forgo any lands, titles and sex for the rest of their lives.

9. The leader of the Maesters is referred to as the Grand Maester and they are the personal Maester of the monarch.

10. The Order of Maesters has a hierarchy:

    i. Novices – new members

    ii. Acolytes – intermediate knowledge

    iii. Maester – advanced knowledge

    iv. Archmaester – expert in a field

11. Archmaesters have a seat on the Conclave which is the council which governs the order and has the power to appoint or remove Grand Maesters.

12. When a Maester learns a new area of knowledge they add a new link to their chain to signify this. The metals and knowledge areas are as follow:

    i.   Black Iron – Ravenry

    ii. Copper – History

    iii. Electrum – Astrology

    iv. Bronze – Astronomy

    v.   Lead – Poison

    vi. Gold – Finance

    vii. Iron – Military

    viii. Steel – Construction

    ix. Pale Steel – Smithery

    x.   Silver – Medicine

    xi. Valyrian Steel - Magic

13. The Small Council is an advisory body to the King or Queen of the Seven Kingdoms.

14. The King or Queen is ultimately responsible for enacting new laws but will often do this upon advice from the Small Council.

15. The Small Council has seven positions which are:

    i. Hand of the King – Chairperson of the council and will serve in proxy for the monarch in their absence

    ii. Master of Coin – Treasurer

    iii. Master of Whispers – Chief spy

    iv. Master of Laws – Chief legal adviser

    v. Master of Ships – Chief naval adviser

    vi. Lord Commander of the Kingsguard – Leader of the Kingsguard

vii.   Grand Maester – Chief Maester

Cersei Lannister added an eighth position which was Master of War but this was later removed.

16. The Kingsguard (or Queensguard) are the monarchs royal bodyguard.

17. The Kingsguard swear an oath to protect the royal family and are required to give up owning any land, taking a wife or fathering any children.

18. Allegiance to any particular house is forbidden for Kingsguard and if the royal house changes, the Kingsguard will move to protect the new monarch. An example of this is Barristan Selmy who was Kingsguard to both Targaryen and Baratheon monarchs.

19. The uniform of the Kingsguard is an all-white cloak and golden armour. This uniform has given rise to the name "White Cloaks".

20. The centre of the Kingsguard is the White Sword Tower which is situated in the Red Keep at Kings Landing.

21. The Lord Commander is the leader of the Kingsguard.

22. The Book of Brothers is a documented history of the exploits of all knights who have served in the Kingsguard and this is updated by the Lord Commander.

23. Daenerys Targaryen has a Queensguard which is formed of close allies and is intended to mimic the function of the Westeros Kingsguard.

24. The Iron Bank of Braavos are the richest organisation in the world.

25. The headquarters of the Iron Bank is in Braavos and situated in the Free Cities of Essos.

26. The symbol of the Iron Bank is two golden triangles one pointing down and the other pointing up. These two triangles overlap to form an hourglass which then had two cupped hands at either side and facing upwards.

27. The Iron Bank stores the deposits within an abandoned iron mine which is sealed using heavy doors and is guarded at all times.

28. The Faceless Men are an assassins guild who are located in Braavos. They get their name because of their ability to change faces and appear as someone else.

29. The Faceless men follow the Many-Faced God and believe that death is a gift to the gods.

30. A person can only be killed by a Faceless Man if it is requested and a price is paid for their death. A Faceless Man cannot therefore, choose who they may or may not kill.

31. Arya Stark leaves the Faceless Men because she is unable to kill for personal gain or out of hate.

32. The Unsullied are elite slave soldiers that are trained in Astapor.

33. Unsullied soldiers begin their training at five years old and train from dusk till dawn. They are also given a puppy which they need to look after and then after one year strangle to death.

34. Only one in four Unsullied soldiers survives the extreme training regime.

35. All Unsullied soldiers are castrated as it is believed eunuchs are more compliant.

36. Upon graduating training an Unsullied warrior must go to the slave market and kill an infant slave.

37. The Brotherhood Without Banners are a group of outlaws whose mission it is to protect the common people of Westeros.

38. The Brothers Without Banners (BWB) was created, albeit not intentionally, by Eddard Stark who sent Beric Dondarrion with a group of soldiers after Ser Gregor Clegane because he killed smallfolk.

39. The Brotherhood are known to worship the Lord of Light.

40. 💣 The Brotherhood Without Banners is also the name used by a group of loyal Game of Thrones fans. GRRM dedicated *A Dance With Dragons* to the Brotherhood Without Banners in their honour.

20. A LAND BEFORE THE SEVEN KINGDOMS

1. Westeros was originally inhabited by two races; the giants of the Dawn Age and the Children of the Forest.

2. Analysis of ancient bones suggests that some giants could have been as tall as fourteen feet.

3. The giants and children of the forest didn't always live in peace. Graves of giants suggest the two were often in conflict.

4. There used to be a land bridge over the narrow sea to the eastern lands. It was this land bridge that the first men crossed.

5. The first men attacked the children of the forest and cut down their weirwood trees until a pact was signed between the two peoples.

6. "The long night" which is referred to often in the books and television shows actually happened during the Age of Heroes and was a cold, dark winter that was said to last a generation.

7. It was during this period that the Starks and Boltons began their age old rivalry. Then, as now, the Starks came out on top!

8. The long night was also when the first recorded sightings of white walkers occurred.

9. Far from Westeros, in the region of Essos, lived the Valyrians who were able to tame the great dragons of that land.

10. The Andals invaded Westeros from West Essos after receiving visions from the seven-faced god. They conquered most of continent except the North and in Dorne.

11. Many of the traditions, language and culture seen in Westeros society in the books and television series are inherited from the Andals.

12. While the battles in Game of Thrones are certainly impressive, they don't compare to the legendary battle between the Rhoynes and the Valyrians. Prince Garin summoned an army a quarter of a million strong to defend the Valyrian attacks but it was futile and ended in tragic defeat.

13. All was not lost for Prince Garin as he called upon the Mother of Rhoyne to avenge their defeat. A fog descended on the land and infected many of the Valyrians with the gruesome disease greyscale.

14. The Valyrian ascent reach a high watermark after the battle of Rhoyne and not long after a cataclysmic eruption of all fourteen flames destroyed the kingdom and its inhabitants in the "Valyrian Doom". Well not all…

15. Deayns the Dreamer of House Targaryen had foreseen the Valyrian Doom and Lord Aenar moved the family to Dragonstone twelve years prior.

16. Aenar brought five dragons to Dragonstone but four died and only one survived, Balerion. The dead dragons did leave behind eggs which resulted in hatching of Meraxes and Vhagar.

17. 💣 **Seven generations later, Aegon Targaryen became the Lord of Dragonstone and began planning his invasion of Westeros. The rest is, as they say, history.**

ABOUT THE AUTHOR

The Fact Bomb Company Limited was created to bring facts to life and present them in a fun and friendly way. We are passionate about facts and we hope our readers enjoy the books that we put together.

Please follow us on social media as we are always keen to hear your feedback about how we can make our product better.

https://www.instagram.com/thefactbombcompany/

https://www.facebook.com/The-Fact-Bomb- Company-334831483939843

https://twitter.com/bomb_fact

https://www.youtube.com/channel/UCmAfXGTX5M98 KoU5tW224jQ?

Any enquiries can be sent to

factbombcompany@gmail.com

THE END